Original title:
Life and Other Things I Don't Understand

Copyright © 2025 Creative Arts Management OÜ
All rights reserved.

Author: Tobias Winslow
ISBN HARDBACK: 978-1-80566-074-3
ISBN PAPERBACK: 978-1-80566-369-0

The Riddle of Our Days

A sock goes missing, it takes a break,
Where does it wander, for goodness' sake?
The toaster's a magician, bread's its trick,
Yet on Mondays, it burns just a bit too quick.

A bird sings loud, thinks it's a star,
While squirrels plot strategies from afar.
Why do we park on driveways, you see,
Then step on the gas to escape with glee?

Unfolding the Unknowable

The cat watches me with eyes of gold,
Plotting revenge for a story untold.
I'm left pondering what schemes it weaves,
While I search for answers in autumn leaves.

The fridge hums secrets in the dark night,
Leftovers shiver from the chilly fright.
Why do we eat what's not meant to be?
A culinary puzzle, just wait and see!

Silhouettes of Curiosity

Why does my phone know me better than friends?
It senses my moods and never pretends.
With thumbs in a race, a swipe and a tap,
I question existence as I take a nap.

The moon's a big cheese in a sky so vast,
It watches our mischief, quite unsurpassed.
With quirks and giggles, the cosmos plays,
Connecting the dots of our silly ways.

Pathways to the Uncharted

In a jammed-up traffic of scattered thoughts,
Who decided that maps could tie us in knots?
Navigating life with a compass of glee,
As I ponder why frogs still hop like me.

Coffee spills softly, a morning decree,
As I fumble through breakfast—oh, how can it be?
The universe chuckles at things we pursue,
While I wonder why socks can't find their clue.

Threads of Enigma

In a world of tangled strings,
My socks seem to have wings.
I search for food, I find a shoe,
Where did all the normal go?

I fumble with my morning brew,
The kettle sings a tune so blue.
I pour too much and hit the floor,
Is this what coffee's for?

Unfolding in the Uncertain Light

In the fridge, a mystery waits,
Is it cheese or some old bait?
I open doors, then shut them fast,
Why does my history never last?

I dance around the laundry pile,
It's a mountain that brings a smile.
Each shirt a tale, each sock a guess,
Whose is this chaotic mess?

The Garden of Half-Understood Truths

My plants are growing, I think they're fine,
But they stare back, like they know the sign.
Water or wine, who can decide?
In this garden, I must hide.

Bees buzzing, they've got their plans,
While I'm just trying the dance of hands.
What's the secret to the bloom?
Is it the sun, or just pure gloom?

Tides of Emotion in Turbulent Seas

I surf the waves of morning news,
Is it dread, or just my snooze?
With every scroll, my heart does race,
A circus in a once calm space.

Cookies crumble, tea spills wide,
Why does calm always go and hide?
I stash my worries in a jar,
Only to lose it, oh how bizarre!

Moments Laced with Confusion

I ask for coffee, get a tea,
The menu says 'just trust me.'
A cat walks in, it takes a seat,
And now I'm puzzled by my feet.

A squirrel offers me a nut,
I wonder if I've lost my cut.
The clouds above begin to dance,
And I just wanted to wear pants.

Reflections in a Murky Pond

I stare into the pond so dark,
My glassy thoughts should leave a mark.
A duck floats by with quite a boast,
I ask it where it likes the most.

It quacks a tune, but I can't tell,
If it's a song or just farewell.
The lilies giggle, steal the show,
I question why they do not grow.

Navigating the Unseen

I trip on air, the ground I punch,
A ninja squirrel claims my lunch.
I try to find a map of dreams,
But all I see are ice cream streams.

The sunlight winks with silly grins,
While shadows argue where to begin.
I dance around an invisible wall,
And then I trip, I take a fall.

The Sounds of Unanswered Queries

I asked a frog for wisdom's call,
It just croaked back, then took a stall.
A bird swoops down, with beak so bold,
It chirps of secrets left untold.

The wind just laughs and blows away,
With riddles wrapped in bright bouquet.
The stars all twinkle, roll their eyes,
As I ponder doughnuts in the sky.

Curiosities That Shape Us

Why do socks always disappear,
Leaving one lonely, full of cheer?
The matching game we cannot win,
Yet here we are, with quite a grin.

Is coffee a friend or cruel foe?
Sipping slowly while we go slow.
With cups and laughs, we claim a prize,
As caffeine giggles in our eyes.

Why do cats insist on naps,
While dogs become our silly chaps?
They rule our hearts with furry charm,
Ensuring we don't come to harm.

What's the deal with the moon's bright glow?
It shines a path for stars to show.
In puzzling ways, it lights our night,
With winks so bold, it feels just right.

The Fabric of Enigmas

Threadbare tales we weave each day,
With fabric quirks that lead astray.
Why do clothes shrink when in a rush?
Worn dreams return to nothing but hush.

Bananas always seem to peel,
In a manner that feels unreal.
They trip us up with each bright smile,
Their slippery charms, a little while.

Time has its own wibbly-wobbly way,
Hours slip by and start to sway.
How can a minute seem like years?
Twirling thoughts lead to laughs and cheers.

Shadows dance like they know the beat,
As we chase them down the street.
With giggles echoing through the air,
The mysteries of days we share.

A Song for the Uninterpreted

Why do we ponder the clouds above?
They shift and sway but fit like a glove.
They hold secrets, whisper low,
Yet keep us guessing, just for show.

What's with the kitchen's rogue drawer?
Filled with gadgets we don't explore.
A can opener lost in a dance,
Among forks and spoons in a trance.

Why do ducks wear such a smile?
Waddling around with style and guile.
They quack with glee, no care for the fuss,
Sharing joy on the paths that we trust.

Can plants really hear when we talk?
Do they giggle when we take a walk?
With leafy ears, they nod along,
In a world where we all belong.

Threads of Consciousness

A puzzle piece we cannot find,
In corners of this wacky mind.
Connections made through silly thoughts,
As giggles bloom in random spots.

What makes the toast land butter side down?
A trick of fate or just a clown?
We laugh and cringe at breakfast time,
In moments sweet, a playful rhyme.

Why does the fridge hum a tune?
A melody that fades too soon.
Dancing treats await our grace,
In a cool spot, they find their place.

Why do we fear the cupboard's creep?
Old ghosts of snacks disturb our sleep.
But laughter echoes with each creak,
In this wild game that we all seek.

Flashes of Insight in the Dark

In shadows I ponder, confused and bemused,
A lightbulb flickers, yet I'm still quite bruised.
Cats stare at me sideways, critiquing my thought,
While I seek out answers, but they're still overwrought.

The toaster's now talking, I swear it's a sign,
It suggests I should slather my bread with some brine.
I argue with furniture, chairs hold their ground,
Yet wisdom eludes me, where is it found?

Thoughts bounce like rubber, so wild and so free,
I chase after them, like a dog up a tree.
The clock's mocking me with its relentless tick,
I laugh at my failures, they're all just a trick.

I raise a glass high, full of wishes and dreams,
To the wonders of nonsense that burst at the seams.
In this carnival ride called the quest to be wise,
I find joy in the laughter that often belies.

The Spectrum of Uncertainty

I paint with confusion on canvases bright,
Each stroke a question, no answers in sight.
A rainbow of chaos, where do I begin?
The shades of my pondering make my head spin.

I argue with colors, they clash and ignite,
Is orange really happy or just overly bright?
With each hue I tackle, the plot thickens more,
The purple's quite shy, but the green wants to roar.

Am I blue with my sorrow or simply too calm?
Does yellow have vitamin or just make me balmy?
The palette's expanding, no boundaries set,
As I whirl in confusion, the spectrum's a pet.

So here's to the colors that dance and collide,
In this abstract existence, I take them with pride.
For in shades of uncertainty, wild and extreme,
I find joy in the chaos, it brightens the scheme.

Tidal Waves of Discontent

The ocean of worries crashes on the shore,
Each wave a concern, like it's keeping score.
I balance on surfboards made of doubt and dread,
Riding through tempests that lounge in my head.

I sip from my coconut, filled with despair,
Seagulls are laughing, they don't have a care.
With every high tide, my patience is thin,
But the sunset is pretty — I guess I'll just grin.

A beach ball of thoughts rolls away from my reach,
It bounces through questions, a chaotic speech.
I contemplate splashes, the foam on the sea,
As the waves keep on crashing, it's just not for me.

Yet in the sea of discontent where I drift,
I search for that treasure, a most precious gift.
It's buried in laughter, beneath worries so vast,
I'll dig through the sand until I find it at last.

Footprints in the Mist

Through cobwebbed conclusions and fogged-over thoughts,
I stumble on pathways that time often plots.
With each careful step, my sandals leave marks,
But the mist swallows clues like it's hiding the sparks.

I wave to the shadows, they chuckle and flee,
They dance in the twilight, like they're teasing me.
With footprints behind me all lost in the haze,
I wonder if wisdom is playing a game.

As I wander through corridors, blank as a slate,
My thoughts tap-dance lightly, they flirt with my fate.
I trip on the echoes of laughter and cheer,
While the mist giggles softly, "You're welcome, dear!"

But I find comfort in wandering far and wide,
In these footprints of blunders, I choose to abide.
For the path is amusing, though shrouded in mist,
Each trip is a treasure that I can't resist.

A Dance with Complexity

In the whirl of oddity, I spin,
With choices that make my head begin.
I trip on logic, laugh and fall,
Yet in this chaos, I stand tall.

Pies in the sky and dreams in the dirt,
I mix up flavors, I dance in a skirt.
The rules of gravity, oh what a jest,
The more I learn, the less I rest.

Questions bounce like balls on a wall,
Answers hide, oh where are they, small?
Each twist and turn is a slip and glide,
In this grand waltz, I take each stride.

So let's embrace the silly and weird,
With confusions that leave us smeared.
In the puzzle of wonders, we all play,
Finding joy in the messy ballet.

Unraveled Knots

Tangled thoughts swarm like bees,
Buzzing loudly, oh do please.
I grapple with strings of my mind,
Yet laughter and chaos are intertwined.

A sock in the dryer, oh where'd it go?
It dances alone, a mystery show.
I search for meaning in cereal oats,
Where's the instruction for life's wild boats?

The cat's in the box, or is it a dream?
Philosophers ponder over the cream.
Why do we worry about things so vast?
When wine and good friends are unsurpassed!

So chuckle at frayed ends and tangles,
To discover joy as the confusion wrangles.
We may not have answers to all we've got,
But we sure know how to laugh at the knot.

The Harmony of What's Missing

In the concert of missing socks and keys,
The rhythm of chaos plays with ease.
Music of questions that float in the air,
As I clap to the beats of my own despair.

The fridge hums secrets I cannot hear,
My pencil's lost, but let's have a beer!
Where is my lunch? Oh goodness me!
A symphony of mishaps, quite splendidly free.

Notes of confusion dance on my tongue,
The tune of the puzzled, forever unsung.
A real-life opera on the stage of my day,
In the gaps of my know-how, come join the fray!

Let the laughter resound where there's little to find,
In the melody of missing, we will unwind.
So raise a toast to the strange and absurd,
For in all that's lost, freedom's conferred.

Whispers of the Unexplained

In the corners of thoughts where oddities reign,
Whispers of nonsense, light as a grain.
Why do we question the tick of the clock?
As I chase after time, I'm told to just walk.

Frogs in tuxedos, they croak in delight,
Explaining the wonders of day and of night.
The universe chuckles, 'Oh, what a show!'
While I'm left wondering, just where did it go?

Riddles and puzzles, all wrapped in a smile,
I ponder for hours, but take a detour awhile.
The light bulb above me flickers and fades,
As I dance through uncertainty, all plans mislaid.

So let's twirl with the whispers, embrace the askew,
In the land of the curious, oh how we flew.
For in each little giggle, there's beauty to find,
In the hush of the funny, where nonsense aligned.

A Tapestry of Inquiries

Why do socks go missing, lost in the wash?
Is there a universe where they all rush?
Do clowns ever get sad, with their big shoes?
And why do cats sit like they own the blues?

Why does my coffee need to be so hot?
Is it the beans or just me that's a lot?
When will I learn that silence isn't gold?
Or is it a treasure, thus left to be sold?

How come the moon's always smiling so bright?
While I struggle to find my left and my right?
Do plants have a secret, whispering way?
Or are they just judging us day after day?

Do fish have regrets, as they swim through the stream?
Or laugh at our worries, like it's all a dream?
Can tickles be captured and stored in a jar?
If so, let's get giggling, we'll raise the bizarre!

The Echo of Untamed Dreams

If daisies could talk, what secrets would spill?
Would they chatter of sunshine, or just keep it chill?
Do crayons get jealous of each other's hue?
Or argue like siblings, all colorful too?

Why does toast always land butter-side down?
Is it plotting revenge on the poor hungry clown?
Do monsters under beds just want to play games?
Or do they have fears, like forgetting their names?

Is cereal a soup when it's swimming in milk?
Or a breakfast hug, soft and smooth like silk?
Why does my phone always die when I'm out?
Is it scheming to keep me from having a shout?

If rainbows had feelings, would they be quite gay?
Or maybe just moody, like clouds on their way?
Do echoes get lonely, lost in the vast space?
Or cheer on their friends with a resonant grace?

When Certainty Meets Doubt

Why do the stars look so close yet so far?
Do they giggle at wishes, or keep them ajar?
Is it true that silence can loudly scream loud?
Or are we just confused, wrapped up in a cloud?

Do my shoes have opinions on where we should tread?
Or do they just follow, to all things I said?
Why do we scribble when we're lost in thought?
While searching for answers that can't be bought?

Can minutes be swallowed, like candy so sweet?
Or do they escape, in a hurried retreat?
If laughter is medicine, what's the right dose?
Should it come with side effects, nobody knows?

Why do we find joy in the silliest things?
Like chasing the breeze or the tune that it sings?
When certainty shows up, does doubt take the day?
Or do they just tango, in a curious sway?

The Enigma of Breathing

What's the secret to having a butterfly dance?
Is it just about wonder, or giving it chance?
Do shadows get lonely when daylight arrives?
Or do they rejoice, while the sun gladly thrives?

Why do we yawn when others begin?
Is it a contagion, or signal to win?
Can hiccups be trained, like a well-behaved pet?
Or are they just rebels, not caring a threat?

Why do we ponder the things we can't see?
Like love in the air or the buzz of a bee?
Is a sneeze a farewell, or a playful hello?
Or a glitch in the matrix, on with the show?

What if our thoughts had a flavor or taste?
Would sweet dreams be berry, or salty with haste?
Can sighs hold the weight of a thousand-day plight?
Or just flutter away, like feathers in flight?

A Compass for the Baffled

Lost in a forest of socks,
Where do they go, oh, who knows?
Goblins may feast on the lost pairs,
Yet I still wear mismatched clothes.

Instructions written in hieroglyphs,
Directions that twist like pretzel bits,
My GPS speaks in riddles so wild,
Is it taking me there, or into the pits?

Clocks tick backward, and time takes a snooze,
Mountains of laundry, I simply refuse.
Under the bed, the dust bunnies hide,
With mysteries ripe and laughter to choose.

Trying to dance on uncertainty's whim,
Spinning around on a question's thin rim.
With socks in the trees and thoughts all askew,
I laugh at the chaos, I'm dancing on a whim.

Mysterious Truths

Why do cats stare at the wall?
Do they see realms hidden from view?
The milk in my cereal has vanished once more,
Was it the dog, or a ghostly boo?

The fridge hums soft like a lullaby,
Ripe lemons giggle, they know the score.
Bananas turn brown as if to conspire,
Pretending they're ripe, but they're really no more.

Tea leaves float like tiny boats,
Every sip brings a capricious chat.
Pouring thoughts like a treacle stream,
What's reliable? Who knows that?

A spoonful of sugar, a dash of the weird,
In a recipe tossed by the kitchen gods.
With spatulas twirling, I ask the great sky,
Where's my remote? Oh, the laughter is broad.

Maps of Uncertainty

A treasure map drawn in crayon hues,
Leads me to places both silly and odd.
X marks the spot where I dropped my keys,
But the treasure's a nap on a comfy pod.

The wind whispers secrets in languages strange,
Clouds are their vessels, fluffy and round.
Do trees hold the answers to questions unsaid?
Or am I just searching for lost socks unbound?

The stars twirl in disco as night takes a peek,
Mapping the cosmos with glitter and glitz.
With each quirk of fate that brings giggles to me,
I scribble my thoughts on a few tangled bits.

So I wander the halls of uncertainty's quest,
Like a grape in a bowl of fruit salad best.
With chuckles and smiles, I embrace what's unknown,
For every odd turn is a treasure confessed.

The Shadows Between Words

In the realm where whispers collide,
I trip on sentences, a clumsy ballet.
A word might disappear, like socks off the line,
Leaving shadows that giggle and play.

The grammar gremlins come out at night,
Turning my phrases into whimsical flubs.
Can a comma be silly? Oh, yes, it can be,
And the periods mostly just sit in the jubs.

Metaphors dance with their feet all askew,
While similes slide down the slippery page.
Each letter a jester with tricks up its sleeves,
In the circus of thoughts, I'm the new stage.

So I leap through the shadows, embracing the fun,
With words as my guide, I'll not overrun.
A jest and a giggle, I tip my hat to the crowd,
For the odd gives me laughter, and I'm far from done.

The Journey beyond the Known.

I walked a path where grass is blue,
Confused by what I thought I knew.
A squirrel asked me for a snack,
I offered him my past backpack.

The sun wore sunglasses, quite a sight,
And danced with shadows, oh what a fright!
I tripped on thoughts, lost in the fray,
Who knew the clouds could float away?

Each step I took was full of cheer,
A nearby lamp post spoke, I fear.
It told me jokes about the moon,
And how it wishes to be a cartoon.

A wise old tree gave me a wink,
Said time flies faster than you think.
So here I stand, a happy fool,
With socks that never match, my rule.

Whispers in the Void

In corners dark, I heard a hum,
It sounded like a distant drum.
A voice that lifted, then it sighed,
Claiming to be the world's best guide.

I asked it where the socks all go,
The voice just laughed, said, "I don't know!"
It whispered secrets of the breeze,
And how it teases unsuspecting trees.

Floating chairs drank tea with glee,
As cookies played hide and seek with me.
What nonsense fills this spooky night,
Yet somehow feels oddly right.

With echoes bouncing off the walls,
I tiptoed through the woozy halls.
The world, a riddle wrapped in a joke,
Even the toaster somehow spoke.

The Puzzle Unraveled

A puzzle box with pieces bright,
My cat arranged them, what a sight!
"Ask not why," she purred so sweet,
"Just know that mice are hard to beat."

Each piece a world, so strange and grand,
One had a castle, one had sand.
I scratched my head, "Which fits where?"
My cat said, "Check under the chair!"

In every corner, laughter hid,
With shapes that wiggled, ran, and slid.
So I just threw the pieces high,
Watched them land, and let out a sigh.

At last, a picture formed from chance,
A circus scene that made me dance.
Yet still it seems I'm out of luck,
The clown's nose is a friendly duck!

Echoes of Invisible Roads

I wandered roads I cannot see,
Where jellybeans grow on a tree.
A fish in boots began to sing,
While I struggled to find my fling.

The stars above had wayward dreams,
And whispered secrets through their beams.
A rollercoaster snake slid past,
Laughing loud, oh what a blast!

Mysteries danced on tiptoe hence,
With riddles that made no sense.
I joined a parade of playful sprites,
As dandelions donned their lights.

In this odd realm of thought and jest,
Where each bizarre twist feels blessed.
I took a step toward the absurd,
And in that moment, joy occurred.

Between Dreams and Realities

In the morning light I look around,
Where socks and keys rarely can be found.
My head spins tales of dragons and gnomes,
While in the kitchen, a toaster moans.

The cat's a philosopher, judging my plight,
As I stumble through coffee, searching for bite.
My reflection chuckles, it feels quite bizarre,
Did I really just dream of a talking jar?

They say reality is quite plain and clear,
But my fridge hums secrets, oh my dear!
A world where plants gossip and socks go to hide,
Yet here I stand, with laundry as my guide.

Maybe tomorrow will make more sense,
But for now, I'll embrace the suspense.
With laughter and oddities tucked tight in my stride,
I'll wander through nonsense, with fears cast aside.

The Weight of Unsaid Words

I swear that the fish in the bowl can hear,
All my musings and snacks — pure volunteer!
Yet I sit in silence, pondering thoughts,
While they plot an escape, my logic in knots.

I could tell my neighbor his garden's a fright,
But he's busy, I think, with a wayward kite.
So I smile and nod, while he toils away,
Is it wrong to be comfy while he goes astray?

There's a taco truck parked just down the street,
But my stomach's too shy, in defeat it retreats.
The menu's a novel, filled with sweet promises,
Yet all I can muster is pumpkin and peas.

So here's to the things left unspoken and still,
To the meals never tried, and the dreams we'll fulfill.
In the awkward silence, my thoughts take a leap,
Wishing I'd been bold, instead of this sheep.

Disguised Journeys

I put on my sunglasses, a hat, and a mask,
Ready to solve the day's tricky task.
But the coffee spills, and I slip on a sock,
Who knew my own home was a toughened block?

Maps pull me in but lead me astray,
As the cat integrally shows me her way.
Every corner turned brings a new surprise,
Like crumbs that conspire to block my eyes.

"Adventure awaits!" the calendar screams,
Yet I end up just cleaning or plotting my dreams.
With a broom as my staff, I conquer the floor,
In this kingdom of chores, who could ask for more?

Still, I'll embrace my haphazard quest,
With mismatched socks and a heart full of zest.
Every stumble and chaos becomes a fine dance,
As I twirl through the madness, just give me a chance.

Fragments of the Unexplained

A spoon once told me it could fly high,
While I scratched my head and said goodbye.
It claimed to have dreams of a life on the moon,
But why does it vanish when I switch to a tune?

The toaster hums softly, an unsung bard,
As crumbs are left behind, it plays life A&R.
It knows all the secrets of burnt toast and jam,
Yet still it sits quietly, an unpainted fam.

There's a parrot who swears it once drove a car,
It squawks of adventures, a true rockstar.
But in reality, it just eats my fries,
Turning my snack into tales and goodbyes.

So I gather these fragments, scattered and bright,
In the oddity of nonsense, I find pure delight.
With giggles and wonders, I'll chase every thread,
In this tapestry woven of whimsy instead.

Nebulas of Thought

In the cosmos of my mind, things float,
Like socks in the dryer, lost in a boat.
I ponder existence, a curious plight,
As clouds of confusion dim the bright light.

Ideas collide, a cosmic ballet,
Like pencils that roll, fading away.
I chase them with glee, though I often fall,
Creating new questions—what's the point of it all?

The planets of wisdom spin in a daze,
While asteroids laugh through their tangled maze.
I scribble my thoughts, but they slip like sand,
With giggles of logic, I don't understand.

Yet in this vast space, I still find delight,
A universe where question marks take flight.
So I toast to the chaos, the mysteries vast,
In the nebulas of thought, I'll forever cast.

Searching for Clarity

Seeking a map in a foggy town,
Where signs point to nowhere and I wear a frown.
A streetlamp flickers, a guide in disguise,
As I wander in circles, much to my surprise.

Like trying to find a matching glove,
In a circus of questions, I push and shove.
Answers are playing hide and seek with me,
In this riddle of oddities, it's hard to see.

With magnifying glasses and a rubber chicken,
I plot my next move, though logic is stricken.
What's the secret code to this great unknown?
Maybe it's laughter, or just a funny bone.

Still I carry on, with a grin so wide,
Searching for clarity in this joyride.
Amidst all the quirks and the curious spins,
I find little treasures where laughter begins.

Diverging Paths of Understanding

Two roads diverged in a puzzling maze,
One led to answers, the other—cliche.
I took the one less traveled, or so I thought,
Only to find that both paths were distraught.

I met a wise owl who just blinked at me,
With riddles so thick, I could hardly see.
He offered me wisdom wrapped in a joke,
But I stumbled and fell, like a bumbling bloke.

Now I walk with a frog who sports a top hat,
His wisdom, like rubber, makes me fall flat.
We hop between choices, with giggles galore,
In the chaos of choice, I begin to adore.

Though the paths may diverge like wild hyperbole,
Together we jump, it's a comical spree.
And in the confusion, I find peace of mind,
In the humor of choices, old truths are redefined.

The Silence of Hidden Answers

In the quiet, answers zip like flies,
They tease and they dance, oh what a surprise!
I whisper my questions, but what do I get?
Just echoes of laughter, in a humorous duet.

The chairs creak with wisdom, but no one is there,
Just shadows and giggles, a comedic affair.
I lean in to listen for secrets concealed,
But they vanish like socks, so cleverly healed.

Searching for whispers in a library vast,
With shelves full of nonsense, I race and I blast.
Hints hide behind novels, they chuckle and cheer,
In this graveyard of thoughts, I'm lost, never near.

But in the silence, a chuckle I hear,
A playful reminder: not all has to be clear.
For answers, dear friend, may wear silly hats,
And the joy of the search can be found where one laughs.

The Language We Never Taught

Words on the tip of my tongue,
But they vanish like socks,
I try to express a simple thought,
Yet it sounds like a flock of rocks.

With every nod, a different tune,
My gestures clash with the phrase,
Who knew my hand could be so rude,
In this dance of silly displays?

Misunderstood at every turn,
My smiles confuse the crowd,
They laugh, I blink, a lesson learned,
In this language loud and proud.

My cat gives me looks of disdain,
As I mumble and fumble words,
Perhaps the real code's in the purr,
Or just in the chaos, absurd.

Dance of the Unfathomable

Twist and twirl, I step on toes,
In a party held by fate,
I never learned the right moves,
But hey, isn't dancing great?

A two-step mixed with a cha-cha,
Salsa's making me dizzy,
The floor spins like a merry-go-round,
While my brain feels all fuzzy.

Waltzing between what's right and wrong,
I trip over bits of wisdom,
Each stumble tells its own strange song,
In life's unpredictable rhythm.

At the end, I bow with a grin,
While the crowd cheers my clumsiness,
Who knew the dance was where to begin,
In this comedy of unpreparedness?

Threads of Uncertainty

I knit a scarf of tangled thoughts,
With yarn that never aligns,
Each stitch is a question, a puzzle,
In colors that don't match signs.

A pattern lost in translation,
As I drop loops left and right,
Yet in the mess, a creation blooms,
A masterpiece of delight.

My needles click with laughter,
As tension rises, then falls,
Who knew chaos could be so warm,
In this fabric of funny brawls?

Each row reveals a new surprise,
A stitch that simply won't obey,
But in the end, it's all a gift,
Even if it leads me astray.

The Map Without a Legend

Here's a map to nowhere, my friend,
With lines that wiggle and squiggle,
X marks the spot? Oh wait, pretend,
I'm lost in this puzzle, no giggle.

Landmarks look like squashed tomatoes,
As I navigate with a whim,
Each corner turned brings new shadows,
And a sense of the absurd within.

Follow the river that runs uphill,
Or the mountain that sinks like a stone,
Who knew that unsure had such a thrill,
In a world where confusion is grown?

I wander through this glorious mess,
With every wrong turn a delight,
Maybe the joy is in the zest,
Of exploring the funny and bright.

Rhythm of the Untold

Ticking clocks and silent phones,
Dance the night, yet feel alone,
Chocolate stains on yesterday's shirt,
Wonders wrap, amidst the dirt.

Mismatched socks and missing keys,
Sipping tea and swatting bees,
The cat just laughed, as I tripped,
The day I swore I'd not be whipped.

Pasta dreams and coffee sighs,
A million laughs, a million cries,
Riding bikes with flat-packed tires,
Catching feels and ducking fires.

A dance with fate, a twist of fate,
Laughter echoes, can't be late,
In this tale of blissful spins,
Who knows where the fun begins?

Shadows of Yesterday

Yesterday's socks parade the floor,
Grocery lists I can't ignore,
Banana peels on my way out,
Living loud without a doubt.

Chasing thoughts like butterflies,
Fluffy clouds and pizza pies,
Thought I saw an alien,
Turns out it's still the mailman.

Silly hats and wild attire,
Bouncing high, a springtime mire,
Fried egg breakfast on my tie,
Giggling at the clouds up high.

A calendar that's upside down,
Painted smiles, a vibrant frown,
Riding waves of quirky schemes,
Living out my wacky dreams.

Mirrors of a Hazy Future

Check the mirror, who's that guy?
Crumbs of toast, oh my, oh my!
Future's foggy, but I see,
A dance of jellybeans and glee.

Monday's tantrum, Tuesday's bling,
Bouncing cats, oh what a fling!
The neighbor's dog barked in tune,
Underneath a plastic moon.

Maps poke fun at my lost ways,
Chasing dreams that dazzle and blaze,
Mistakes have more fun than the right,
As I drift into the night.

The clock mocks, ticks ever so slow,
Where I end up? No one knows,
Scribbled hopes in crayon hues,
Life's a joke in mismatched shoes.

Epiphanies at Twilight

Twilight whispers, 'What's the plan?'
Sunset sparkles on the pan,
I pour my thoughts like silly beans,
Wondering, where's the in-betweens?

The pine trees nod their leafy heads,
While I'm tangled in my threads,
A squirrel tells me secrets sly,
As I wave at the passing sky.

Brain like jelly, thoughts that hop,
With every question, a quirky plop,
A tarantula at my tea party,
Who knew bugs could be so hearty?

With every chuckle, I'm bit by wit,
Life's wild dance; I just won't quit,
Under stars, the humor's bright,
In this jumble, twilight's light.

Chasing the Invisible Thread

I held a string that led nowhere,
Tangled in thoughts, I despair.
The cat meows, unaware of my plight,
As I chase a shadow in the dimming light.

A squirrel scoffs from the nearby tree,
Who knew it spoke fluent absurdity?
I trip on my brain, what a silly dance,
While the coffee mug offers me no second chance.

Calendars mock with each passing day,
Time's just a joke that won't go away.
I search for treasure that is lost in a grin,
But the x-marks-the-spot is beneath my chin.

So I laugh at the riddle, the twist and the turn,
Perhaps it's a lesson that I still need to learn.
With a wink from the universe, I'll play this charade,
Chasing the invisible, I'm happily swayed.

When Certainty Meets Ambiguity

I woke up today with a grand plan,
But my sock has vanished, oh where is it, man?
My breakfast has ideas of its own,
Turning toast into a hesitant scone.

The sun's playing hide-and-seek with gray,
Clouds giggle softly, come out to play.
Yesterday's wisdom slips like a fish,
I'm searching for meaning in a jelly dish.

A bird on the fence squawks 'what's the fuss?'
While I ponder meaning in existential dust.
Should I trust the wind? Should I follow the breeze?
Maybe just stick to my cozy, warm teas.

So I juggle my thoughts like a clown on a stage,
With questions that feel like an open cage.
When certainty knocks, do I open the door?
Or send it away with a soft 'nevermore'?

The Riddle of Existence

I peek into mirrors that only reflect,
A face full of nonsense, what should I expect?
Puzzles in corners, all asking for light,
While the cat chooses now for her nighttime flight.

The stars whisper secrets, see how they shine,
But their answers are muddled, not one single line.
I ask the goldfish, it swims in a circle,
It knows something, but keeps its thoughts verbal.

A spoon claims it's forked in a heated debate,
While knifes roll their eyes, feeling quite late.
I ponder the questions from dawn until dark,
But the light flickers off, calling me a shark.

The riddle spins round like a vinyl on play,
As I'm dancing with doubts in a most awkward ballet.
With each twist and turn, I chuckle and glide,
In this maze of confusion, I take it in stride.

A Symphony of Question Marks

The kettle whistles tunes unknown,
While I sip from a cup made of stone.
Chairs seem to giggle with thoughts of their own,
As the rug rolls its eyes at my bother-crowned throne.

Pages in books whisper riddles at night,
The words dance away, just out of my sight.
A cat-sized magician pulls thoughts from the air,
I'm the audience lost in deep layers of flair.

The clock strikes a tune that's both wrong and right,
Each tick is a laugh trailing off into night.
I join in the chorus of questions and sighs,
As the ceiling spins tales, though I'm not quite wise.

So here's to the symphony, chaotic and grand,
Where confusion conducts and we all take a stand.
With each note of laughter a truth's revealed,
In this orchestra of oddity, my fate is sealed.

Fragments of Clarity Amidst Chaos

In a world that's upside down,
My socks refuse to match, somehow.
I ponder stars and sandwich toast,
While my cat stares, we know not how.

Thoughts jump like frogs in a pond,
Chasing flies of fleeting dreams.
I scribble notes, but lose my pen,
And wonder what that even means.

The clock ticks loud, a mocking sound,
As coffee spills on yesterday's mess.
I laugh along, embrace the swirl,
Amidst the chaos, I find less stress.

With every puzzle piece I trace,
A hundred questions fill the air.
But who really found the missing part?
Just ask the cat—she doesn't care!

The Dance of Questions and Answers

Why does my toast land butter-side down?
Who invented the word 'pundemic'?
I question life's grand cosmic joke,
While wearing shoes that don't quite fit.

I twirl in circles, a dizzy dance,
Just like my thoughts on a windy day.
Answers chase me like a lost dog,
Barking 'fetch it!' then running away.

Do plants know when we talk to them?
Or is it just me in a garden dream?
I try to fathom this spinning world,
Yet I laugh aloud at how it might seem.

At parties, I ask the weirdest things,
Like, 'Do aliens like ice cream cones?'
The answers never seem quite clear,
Yet in the fun, I feel at home.

Reflections in a Foggy Mirror

I stood before my foggy glass,
With toothpaste smudges on parade.
Who is that marvelous stranger there?
Oh wait, it's just the morning cascade.

I'm like a puzzle with missing bits,
Each piece a bit off-center still.
But laughter bubbles through the cracks,
As I embrace the cheerful thrill.

My hair's a nest of wild design,
As I try to decipher this face.
Is that a wrinkle or a laugh line?
I shrug it off; I'm still in the race.

In other reflections, sometimes bright,
I glimpse the weight of heavy thoughts.
Yet there's a wiggle, a silly grin,
And I'm reminded joy can't be bought.

Bridges Built on Hesitation

I tiptoe on a rickety bridge,
Constructed of doubts and silly fears.
One step forward, then two back,
While counting all my missing peers.

Will I jump or will I wait?
Like stones tossed in a sleepy brook.
The ripples raise a thousand doubts,
As my mind's the best nosy cook.

Friends nudge me gently to just leap,
But what if I splash and make a mess?
With a laugh, I finally let go,
And bounce right back; oh, what a dress!

Bridges sway, but I find my groove,
In hesitation, I discover glee.
For life is nothing but a funny trail,
Where every misstep leads to me!

The Puzzle of Every Breath

Each morning I wake up so bright,
Only to find socks on my right.
What do they do when I'm not near?
Waltz with each other? Oh dear!

The toast burns while I brew my tea,
Yet somehow it keeps calling me.
Is the kettle giggling in delight?
Or is that just me, alone tonight?

Why do calendars always confuse?
They flip and twirl, play with my snooze.
Days run faster than a dog on a spree,
Or is it just my endless coffee spree?

With every chuckle, a riddle escapes,
Baffling thoughts in all of their shapes.
I dance with questions, a merry charade,
In this puzzling play, I'm happily swayed.

Whispers in the Unknown

Beneath the bed, what lurks and waits?
Dust bunnies plotting to change my fate.
Do they hold secrets of the grand unseen?
Or just my snacks, unsharply gleaned?

I talk to my plants, do they reply?
With leaves that flutter, oh my, oh my!
If they could giggle, what tales would they tell?
Of dance parties held, and meals that fell?

The cat thinks she owns this domain,
Plotting her reign, it drives me insane.
With each soft purr, does she know, I ask?
What's under the surface, a curious task?

Whispers echo down the hall,
Turns out it's just my wall clock's call.
I laugh at the oddities shaping my day,
Who knew the mundane could lead me astray?

Echoes of a Confounded Heart

My heart skips beats like a game of hopscotch,
Is it love, or just me, feeling the botch?
Chocolate crumbles tie my heart in knots,
With each silly crush, my logic rots.

I trip on words when you're around,
Like clumsy feet dancing on shaky ground.
Are these butterflies? Or a wild moth swarm?
Why does my smile break every norm?

Notes from a crush float up on a breeze,
Whispers of questions that bring me to tease.
If laughter could answer, I'd surely know,
Why this feeling takes over, steals the show.

Though my heart is confused, I'll wing it each day,
With giggles and grins, I'll find my way.
For if this is puzzling, so be it my art,
Embracing each echo of this baffled heart.

Navigating the Unseen Currents

In the ocean of thoughts, I'm a tiny boat,
Drifting through waves that seem to gloat.
What's that shadow beneath me, I wonder?
A fishy philosopher, perhaps with blunder?

Maps are just scribbles when I'm lost at sea,
Navigating the whims of me, oh me!
I turn left at laughter, then right at the sighs,
Caught in a squall of bewildered tries.

If only the stars could send me a note,
On how to sail smoothly, instead I float.
With a wink from the moon as my guiding light,
Adventures ensue in the thick of the night.

So I'll ride the currents, laugh at the storm,
Find joy in the chaos, that's my norm.
For in the depths of confusion and fun,
I'll navigate mysteries, one silly pun.

Habitations of the Paradox

In a world of silly jest,
Where ducks wear hats and jesters rest,
I chase my thoughts like buzzing flies,
While pondering the truth in pies.

A cat plays chess, it wins by chance,
And I'm confused by its advance.
With every move, my logic bends,
A game with rules that have no ends.

The toaster sings a morning tune,
As waffles dance beneath the moon.
I'm stuck there, grinning wide and bright,
Thinking I might join the kite.

The cat, the toast, the juggling deer,
All reveal things that I hold dear.
In silliness, the truth resides,
Found in the quirks my brain decides.

Murmurs of a Conflicted Soul

A chicken crossed to find some peace,
While I just ponder why, and cease.
Eggs mostly crack without a fuss,
While I keep asking, why the rush?

Invisible friends at dinner speak,
Their conversations are quite bleak.
I laugh along, they jest and poke,
Yet leave me wondering if it's a joke.

The sock drawer hides a missing shoe,
And offers secrets that feel so true.
If only I could ask it why,
But it just sighs and rolls an eye.

Where thoughts collide in awkward sum,
And conundrums hum a silly drum.
I wade through questions, fair and foul,
In search of sense, I feel quite sole.

The Canvas of Unresolved Thoughts

I dip my brush in shades of glee,
To paint the world that's strange to me.
Each stroke's a riddle wrapped in fun,
With colors blending, not just one.

A squirrel debates with the old oak tree,
While I ponder what could possibly be.
The leaves just giggle, hum, and sway,
As I chase thoughts that drift away.

The canvas spills its vibrant plight,
Where fireflies dance and tease the night.
A masterpiece that's quite absurd,
Yet all agree it's quite a word.

I step back, scratching my head,
What does it mean? I just don't dread.
For in this mess, a spark remains,
That tickles the heart, and curiously reigns.

Jigsaw Pieces of Illumination

A puzzle with a missing piece,
I scramble 'round but find no lease.
The cat just swipes the colors blue,
While I miscount my thoughts anew.

Each fragment shouts, "Hey, look at me!"
While I'm confused by the loud decree.
The edges, they seem far away,
Lost in the middle of bright dismay.

Mismatched socks gather for a cause,
As I unwind these silly flaws.
The sun a jigsaw, shines and glows,
Puzzle-piece hearts where laughter flows.

In tangled thoughts, a light appears,
That tickles me and stirs my fears.
Perhaps the chaos's meant to blend,
In this strange dance that knows no end.

Flickers of Awareness

I dropped my phone, it lit up bright,
A message from the world, a cosmic bite.
But what it said, I still can't tell,
Maybe just spam, or a wish from a shell.

I spilled my tea, it danced and swirled,
A liquid ballet in my cluttered world.
Do cups have feelings? I ponder and grin,
While cleaning up stains that gather within.

A parking ticket tucked in the door,
Telling me I might be poor.
Do machines judge how I live my day?
Or just patrol in a robotic way?

I plant my dreams in a cup of earth,
Water them gently, await their birth.
Will they sprout thoughts or merely weeds?
In my garden of hopes, I scatter the seeds.

Ciphers of Existence

A rubber band flicks my sleepy brow,
What cosmic force made me wonder how?
Rubber is stretchy, but so is my mind,
It snaps, it rebounds, it's truly entwined.

A cat on the fence thinks it owns the street,
With a strut and a saunter, a rhythmic beat.
I wave at the creature in bemusement,
Does it know I'm here? What's its amusement?

Why do socks vanish in the wash?
Is there a black hole with a fashionable posh?
I'll knit a pair from my old despair,
Fashionable comforts, beyond compare.

An email comes; it's marked "urgent"
About a lost kite or a trendy detergent.
I chuckle and wonder who writes this stuff,
As I surf through nonsense, it's never enough.

The Art of Wandering

I took a stroll in my own backyard,
Met a gnome who looked quite frazzled and marred.
He whispered secrets of the flowers' plight,
While I tripped on grass; oh, what a sight!

In a café, I ponder a dish that's served,
Is this cheese or a truly weird nerve?
My taste buds dance while my brain just swings,
At least the coffee is boosting my zing.

Chasing my shadow, it runs away fast,
I play tag with thoughts, but they never last.
Do they laugh at my efforts? Maybe they know,
That wandering minds sometimes put on a show.

The clouds above seem to gather and fuss,
I shout at them softly, "Don't cause a fuss!"
They rain down laughter, I slip and slide,
Who knew the sky would join in my ride?

A Melody for the Unknown

I whistle tunes that float in the air,
Notes chase each other, a playful affair.
But what is the point? I often forget,
Yet my heart keeps drumming, a joyful duet.

The elevator talks with its ding and its hum,
I chat back politely, "Oh, how you're glum!"
Does it wish for a day out, a walk on the street?
Or is it content, just moving my feet?

Cooking dinner, I dance with the pan,
A spatula twirls like a cool disco fan.
Why do veggies giggle when sautéed with flair?
In my kitchen of chaos, it's all in the air.

The clock on the wall ticks with a grin,
As I ponder the wonders I never begin.
What's next on this journey of curious jest?
Perhaps it's just laughter that leads me to rest.

The Intrigue of the Everyday

I once saw a cat wearing a hat,
It strutted with flair, what's up with that?
A squirrel rode by on a tiny bike,
With wheels so small, it looked like a strike.

The toast popped up, a surprise indeed,
It landed so funny, a breakfast creed.
My coffee was dancing; I swear it swayed,
I think it had dreams on which it played.

A sock went missing, who knows where it fled?
The vacuum's a thief, or so it's said.
As I ponder these things, I can't help but chuckle,
For each day's a riddle, a joyful muckle.

With friends we debate what the sky might mean,
Perhaps it's a canvas for God's paint machine.
We laugh till we cry, in this puzzling spree,
At the whims of the world, so silly and free.

Fleeting Moments of Clarity

I tripped on a shoelace, so neatly tied,
And wondered if shoes have a secret guide.
The shine of my phone calls for attention,
Yet it's my cat that sparks the most apprehension.

In the fridge, a pickle waved goodbye,
As my leftover pizza tried to comply.
The lights flickered twice, was it ghosts or the fuse?
In this typical mayhem, what's there to lose?

I spotted a fly that looked quite profound,
Reflecting on purpose while spinning around.
I pondered aloud, "Are we all just here?
Or simply a jest from a cosmic sphere?"

These moments, they flit like leaves in the breeze,
Sometimes full of nonsense, yet I find them a tease.
In the chaos of days filled with quirks and with glee,
I capture the whims and just let them be.

The Beauty of Nebulous Thoughts

A cloud shaped like a burger drifted by,
While I hoped for answers from the popcorn sky.
The rules of the universe seem to bend,
When I start to think, "What's around every bend?"

Pants on the line look like they're dancing,
Do they wiggle for joy, or just take a prancing?
The wind whispers secrets, yet I'm left in the dark,
As I spy on a squirrel, perfecting its arc.

A shirt on a chair speaks volumes of style,
Though I can't quite recall when I last wore a smile.
In the grocery store, veggies roll with glee,
As I wonder which one holds the key to the sea.

Thoughts bubble and burst, like soda in flight,
Chasing ideas that vanish from sight.
In this world of confusion, a chuckle's the cure,
For the beauty of nonsense is perfectly pure.

Beyond the Edge of Understanding

I saw a dog dressed as a hot dog today,
Wagging its tail like it's here for a play.
The fish in the tank swim in circles so grand,
While plotting their escape from this watery land.

An onion just cried while I chopped it in half,
And I laughed at its tears, like it told a joke half.
The microwave dinged, was it time for a show?
Or just the leftovers wanting a glow?

The toaster came alive, its pop like a cheer,
What advice could it give if only it could steer?
As I sit here in wonder, the questions arise,
Do objects with character see through our eyes?

With each silly thought that floats on the breeze,
I glance at the mundane and find it a tease.
In this realm of confusion, I joyfully dance,
For the world's just a riddle, full of happenstance.

Secrets Beneath Ordinary Skies

Underneath the quiet stars,
A sock is lost, a treasure far.
Behind the couch, it hides away,
Laughing at our frantic play.

The cat knows all the secret paths,
While birds critique our silly laughs.
They chirp advice, yet we ignore,
The laundry piles forever more.

Rain falls lightly on the ground,
It washes off the thoughts unbound.
Puddles form, a dance to share,
As sloshing feet forget their care.

In dreams, we chase the silly things,
Like searching for a bird that sings.
Yet morning comes, the song is gone,
And so we greet another dawn.

Chasing Shadows and Sunbeams

Chasing shadows on the floor,
They stretch and yawn, then ask for more.
Sunbeams tease with a playful kiss,
A game of hide, a moment's bliss.

The clock ticks loud, a sneaky thief,
Takes time away, as if in grief.
Yet here we sit, just wasting days,
In comfortable, unfocused ways.

A butterfly lands on my nose,
It giggles softly, then off it goes.
While rabbits blink with winks of mirth,
As if to say, "What's this all worth?"

We stumble through, with constant dread,
Of missing all the things we've said.
Yet laughter lingers in the air,
And lightness bends beyond compare.

When Time Falls Asleep

When time takes naps, it snores aloud,
And dreams of days lost in the crowd.
The minutes twirl in sweet ballet,
As hours drift and sway away.

A drowsy sun hums lullabies,
While shadows blink their sleepy eyes.
An afternoon is often cruel,
Lost in thought or silly duel.

Countless seconds slip and slide,
Like sneaky fish, they gently hide.
Yet here we sit with cups of tea,
And ponder what's the mystery.

The moon giggles, the stars conspire,
All while we sit and slowly tire.
In the daze of dreams that swirl,
We wonder what in time's the pearl.

Questions Beneath the Surface

What's the secret of that tree?
It whispers, sways, and looks at me.
With wisdom wrapped in leaves so green,
It laughs at things I've never seen.

Beneath the rug, a mystery waits,
Collecting crumbs, it surely states:
"Life's a puzzle, I hold the keys,
But who will ask, or bend their knees?"

The dog just barks, he doesn't care,
To him, each moment's an open air.
Yet cats in corners watch with grace,
As if they've known a better place.

So here we giggle, chase and muse,
In life's great game, we choose to lose.
With silly wonders round each bend,
We'll laugh through all, and call it zen.

www.ingramcontent.com/pod-product-compliance
Lightning Source LLC
Chambersburg PA
CBHW072139200426
43209CB00051B/157